Linda!
Thanks for your
enthusiastic support
of my work!

:) Jerilynn Henrikson

SEVEN
TO
ONE

———

*My Life
Measured in
Dog Years*

———

Jerilynn Jones
Henrikson

Rowe Publishing

ISBN 13: 978-1-939054-51-7

Chapter heading photos used by permission courtesy of family members and friends of the Author.

1 3 5 7 9 8 6 4 2

Printed in the United States of America
Published by

Rowe Publishing
www.rowepub.com
Stockton, Kansas

*These stories are dedicated to any of my
ex-students who said to me,
"Mrs. H, you should write a book."*

Well I did, and here it is.

*Read it, and write a five paragraph, double
spaced critique by Friday. Remember to use
specific examples to support your ideas.*

*Send your paper to
jerilynnh@yahoo.com.*

Contents

Preface

*T*radition has it that one year of a dog's life is equal to seven years of human life. The lifespan of the average dog is about twelve years. It follows that in eighty-four years a person could sequentially share life with seven dogs. My goal here is to "tell my life" in dog years, to measure phases of my existence by the lives of the dogs that have shared it. Of course, this is a thinly disguised excuse to tell stories about the humans who have shared my life as well. Are these stories true? Mostly. Exaggerated? Possibly. Engaging? Hope so.

The Grandmothers' Dogs

My sister, Mary Beth, and I share our pool with Skipper.

The first dogs in my life weren't really mine. Skipper the mutt belonged to my mom's parents, and Ginger the springer ran the residence where my dad grew up.

Mom's parents lived on Cottonwood Street in Emporia, Kansas. Their two-story, square white house was probably one of those homes ordered as a kit from Sears or Montgomery Ward back in the 30s.

One afternoon after school, my grandmother looked out the front window to see her youngest, Franklin D, pulling a white dog up the sidewalk by a rope tied to its neck. Once on the porch, he took off the rope, tossed it into the spirea bushes, picked up the pooch, and came into the living room. "This dog followed me home. Can I keep him?" Grandma caved and the dog stayed. Frankie named him Skipper. A circus had recently put on a show at the civic auditorium just down Sixth Avenue. We thought Skipper might have been left behind. He knew lots of tricks. He was mostly white, perhaps part spitz, and medium sized. A bit longer than tall, he might have been part corgi. He was tolerant of kids. My mom used to have a picture of me at about eight months with Skipper under the coffee table sharing his bone. I was his first "grandchild" but seventeen more followed.

Grandma Martha worked at Bon Ton Cleaners and made "smashed" potatoes and fried chicken. From her I learned to eat. I have often wished I had also learned her passion for cleaning dirt. She did not clean; she attacked. She preached that any good housewife had all her "chores" done by nine a.m. This included baking pies and bread, making beds, sweeping, mopping, scrubbing, and doing the laundry. She came to visit me early one morning and was thrilled to see my laundry on the line by eight. I didn't have the heart to tell her I had hung it there a little past noon three days before.

Grandpa Barney was a welder, a Democrat (Yes there are some in Kansas. Who else would name his son Franklin D?), and a Yankee fan. From him I learned to swear. Skipper thought his name was Dammit Skipper, Get Your Ass in Here! The more grandpa swore at him, the harder he wagged his tail.

Grandma Martha had some creative ways to involve in the housework, any grandkid she happened to be babysitting. My favorite was helping to wax the linoleum. After applying the wax, she would let it dry, and then get a kid to help with the buffing. This involved a fuzzy dust mop and a child small enough to straddle and ride it around the floor while granny swung it in circles and arcs with Skipper chasing and yapping. We cousins thought it was more fun than a rollercoaster.

Perhaps my favorite story about Grandma Martha's tidiness happened shortly after hubby Duane and I returned from his military stint in San Antonio. When we moved, we left our parakeet, Linus, with her until our two-year tour was up. She adored Linus. He was a special bird. He could talk. His vocabulary included here kitty, kitty, kitty, Duane is a fink, hello, come here, bye now. But what grandma liked best about him was his personal hygiene routine. He took a bath every morning in his green plastic bathtub with a mirror in the bottom. Then he would check out his reflection in the toaster, bobbing his head, and muttering to himself in parakeet. When we came home from Texas and reclaimed Linus, grandma went directly to the pet store and bought a bird that looked just like him. This one was, however, in grandma's words, "a dud." He didn't talk, but worse, he refused to bathe. No shape or color of tub or bowl, or temperature of water would tempt him.

She named him Billy. One day when I came for a visit, I stepped up to the cage to say hi to Billy. He went berserk. I asked grandma what was wrong. She said, "He's been like that ever since his bath."

"But I thought you said he didn't like to take a bath," I said.

"He doesn't, she answered, "so I gave him one."

"How in the world did you do that?" I asked, wondering how one would go about force-bathing a bird.

"I just put a little shampoo and water in the bottom of a fruit jar, put him in, put on the lid, and shook him up a little."

I gave her a brief lecture on parakeet husbandry explaining that not ALL parakeets enjoy bathing, and that obviously Billy was of that category. He eventually recovered his trust in humankind, but he never learned to talk or take a bath. He remained a "dud" until the end of his days.

Grandma Lehnherr barely remembered her mother, who died in childbirth when she was just two years old. Her father had vowed to his dying wife that he would never remarry. Perhaps this explains grandma's devotion to keeping a tidy home and cooking delicious food for all those kids and grandkids: compensation for the unwashed clothes and skimpy meals of childhood. Among us cousins were a Jeri, a Mary, a Larry, and a Perry. When grandma got older, she would often go through this whole list before she hit the right name. Sometimes in frustration she would add "Damnit" to the list. Whenever she did, Skipper came a'running.

My dad's family lived in Topeka on Wabash Street, north of the Kansas River. His home was pointy and Victorian, covered with gingerbread trims and flanked by three porches. My Grandmother Jones lived with her mother, Lisbeth Oliver Stroup Clingan, known to me as Mo. The rest of her family, especially her two sisters, Minnie and Mae, called her Lizzy. By the time I appeared on the scene, Mo was in her late 80s and had outlasted two husbands. She lived to be ninety-seven, mostly I think to avoid relinquishing power over her poor widowed daughter, my grandmother, Gertrude Jones. When I was about eight, I wrote the following poem about Grandma Jones:

My grandma has the whitest hair and the bluest eyes.

She makes me noodles and apple pies.

Her voice is soft just like her lap,

And she cuddles me cozy when I take

my nap.

Short and portly, Grandma Gertie reminded me of the clucky hens she kept in the old stable on the alley. She always wore a corset, opaque hose and dresses, and stacked heel lace-up shoes. Any time she went out, she added a hat and gloves. Her walk was amazingly recognizable and seems to pass to her great-great-grandchildren as they take their first steps—short steps, chin up, chest out, shoulders up, elbows back. You almost expect to see them, like those hens, stop, scratch the ground, and search for bugs.

Mo and her dog Ginger, a geriatric orange and white springer spaniel, ran a tight ship. I think Ginger was in her late 80s too. By the time I knew her, Ginger had zero tolerance for small children. She growled and snapped whenever I got within touching distance and spent most of her time sleeping among the pots of amaryllis in the window seat. She also had a raging case of halitosis and a huge ugly oozing mass between the toes of her right front foot. In all fairness, it might have been a good relationship if I had known Ginger when she was a pup, or if Mo had loosened the strings on her old black purse and taken out a few bucks for some veterinary care. Of course, these were different times when it came to health care for dogs.

Both of my grandmothers were amazing women. They were both excellent cooks and skilled in the art of gardening and canning what they produced, important survival skills during the Great Depression. They had an important influence on me because they were both talented story spinners. I loved hearing tales of their growing-up years and credit them with teaching me the power and beauty of well-chosen words. Grandma Jones was as quiet and kind as Grandma Lehnherr was feisty and enthusiastic, a lovely balance for a young personality.

Skipper taught me to love dogs; Ginger taught me that all dogs do not love me.

2

California and Spike

Spike, father "unknown"

My parents found a puppy for me for my third birthday. By then, we lived on 111th Street in Los Angeles where we moved from Kansas after my dad returned from fighting Hitler. His brother-in-law got him a job at the Jantzen Swim

Suit factory. After the war, he returned to Emporia to live with mom and me in a little blue Victorian cottage on Exchange Street. He had a hard time holding a job, losing eight different positions in two years. When Harold Leroy Jones enlisted in the army, he was barely twenty and looked fifteen—five foot seven and one hundred twenty pounds. The war left deep psychological and emotional scars. For years he suffered night terrors. He had achieved the rank of sergeant, was a small arms specialist, and commanded a tank in the Battle of the Bulge, where his tank took a direct hit. He survived but his crewmen did not. Perhaps this explains why he never wanted a job that included authority over other workers.

In LA, my mother, Ida Lena Lehnherr Jones, nicknamed "Tooie," worked as a registered nurse at small maternity hospital near our home. Evie, my mom's youngest sister, and Dorothy and Lucile, my dad's sisters, provided daycare. My memories of those days consist of an odd collection of disconnected details and are probably highly influenced by listening to family talk of these times and looking at those old black and white snapshots with the serrated edges. My aunt Evie was just twelve years older than I. She babysat me during the summers when she was not in school. She has always contended that I was a spoiled brat. There is some evidence, I must admit, in that direction. My mother had a professional photographer come to the house regularly to take my picture. I was cute. I look in the mirror now and wonder what happened. Evie said I used to tell my mom every day when she came home from work, "Aunt Evie spanked my butt," whether she had or not.

Aunt Dorothy and Aunt Cile were both married, but never had children. They absolutely doted on our family. Even after we moved back to Kansas, they were just a phone call or train ride away. They took us in almost every summer and entertained us with all Southern California had to offer: Disneyland, Knotts Berry Farm, Marine Land, The La Brea Tar Pits (or Par Tits as Aunt Dot called them) and of course, the beach.

I used to love the days when Aunt Dot babysat. She was a person of amazing innocence and sweetness, a master of misspeak and constant victim of teasing from her ornery brother, my dad. Once for breakfast at the local greasy spoon, she ordered Number Two with Pisscuits. Part of our ritual when she came to baby sit was to take a bubble bath before my nap. She would bring paper packets of gardenia-scented bubble powder that filled the bathtub with fragrant, foamy mounds. One day she put off bath time saying that we needed to wait for the Postal Express man. She was expecting a package. I thought she meant that he was going to join us in the bath.

When he rang the doorbell, I ran to answer the door. (Of course, Aunt Dot had to hurry to put Spike, my puppy, in the bedroom because he would try to eat anyone in uniform.) "Oh boy," I gushed. "Are you going to take a bubble bath with Aunt Dorothy and me?"

He looked over my head at a shapely, embarrassed Aunt Dot and leered, "Well, I guess that's up to Aunt Dorothy!"

Our house was a tiny, cute bungalow with living room, dining room, kitchen, two bedrooms and a pink tiled bath. The drive way consisted of two strips of concrete with grass between. Three tree roses trimmed the front entry, a peach tree competed with Spike for space in the fenced back yard, and a pink oleander dominated the small front lawn. The flowers on that bush smelled like sugar cookies. My mother warned me that they were poisonous and that I should not eat them. Of course, I would never have thought of eating flowers if she had not mentioned it.

The Oliveras lived on one side. Their rainbow colored bungalow overflowed with beautiful brown children who brought home tortoises every time they came back from a weekend trip to the desert. Mr. Baker and Mrs. Cook (or vise versa, I never could remember) lived on the other side. They had a Chihuahua that played the piano. I was fascinated by that dog and puzzled by the disparity in the owners' last names. I never did get a satisfactory answer to my questions about that.

My other memories of the place include a neighborhood kid with blond hair who came to play on occasion. We would stretch out on our bellies on the floor and color in a coloring book. I was frustrated by the fact that he was meticulous and slow, and I was always ready to turn the page before he was.

I also remember a neighborhood theater, The Riveola, which played westerns. I was in love with Roy Rogers. My mom and Aunt Cile took me to see him at Bullocks department store. We followed a noisy serpentine line of harried parents and impatient kids winding through make-up counters, racks of shoes, and clothing carousels for what seemed like hours and finally made it to Roy. I pitched a huge fit when all I got was a pat on the head. I wanted to talk about Trigger and Bullet and Dale and invite them all to dinner. Never mind the 1,987 kids in line behind us.

Aunt Cile, wise, witty, and fun, loved to take us to the beach. Her hubby, Uncle Johnny was her perfect match. Once while we were bobbing in the surf, a big wave knocked off the top of her two-piece. Uncle Johnny said, "Lady, if you're going to drown those puppies, I'll take the one with the pink nose."

Anyway, back to my dog, Spike. (Obviously, I am prone to digression...probably ADD. My mom did get a note from the kindergarten teacher, brief and to the point: "Your daughter is restless on her rug.") The birthday dog was acquired from a newspaper ad: "small mixed-breed puppies to give away." My parents have always been naive about animals. They saw the mother, a small terrier type, but the father was "unknown." We named the pup Spike and he promptly grew into the name. Dollars to donuts the dad was a pit-bull. Spike had a square head, no neck, a fireplug body, and he waddled like a weightlifter. His coat was a lovely yellow and brown bristly brindle. He loved me and hated anyone wearing a uniform: meter readers, cops, and mailmen. We got warning letters from all three departments. The mailman was especially testy. Part of his attitude was probably my fault because I routinely filled the mailbox with snails.

3

Back to Kansas

Mom, Mary, and Jeri at Plymouth

Iwas perfectly happy with 111th Street but my parents decided we should move back to Kansas. Aunt Dot and Uncle Roy bought the place and lived there for many years. I'm sure that is why my memories of the house and neighborhood remain vivid. We loaded the Chevy and headed east. I shared the backseat with Spike and a blonde console radio. Crossing the desert with no air-conditioning and a short-nosed dog in close quarters involved much panting, snorting, and slobber. Spike and I took turns napping among the legs of the radio and drinking 7-up from a paper cup.

We moved into an old farmhouse about eight miles from Emporia in a small village called Plymouth. Spike had a tough time adjusting to life in the country. He killed the neighbor's chickens and chased cows. Then he disappeared. My Uncle Bud told me he had run away.

The community of Plymouth was home territory. My grandparents had lived there when their children were small. Grandpa Lehnherr ran a service station up on Highway 50. I've often wished I had the hand-lettered placard he placed in the window: "I'll pump your gas, I'll mind your baby. But I only take cash, and I don't mean maybe." He could have written for BurmaShave. Another of his poems was a bit more salty. Each morning, my grandmother served him his coffee with the sugar bowl and a small tin of condensed milk. Next to the milk can she placed a punch type can opener. As he punched a hole in the tin, he always said, "No tits to pull, no hay to pitch. Just poke a hole in the sonofabitch."

My mom's brother my Uncle Bud and his wife Aunt Betty lived with us for a time. The antics of him and my dad are the stuff of legend in Plymouth. The neighbors had this black cow that was always getting out of their pasture and tromping other people's tomatoes. My dad and Uncle Bud caught her and made a Holstein out of her with some whitewash. The neighbors drove up and down the roads searching for their cow, but they didn't find her until it rained.

Our neighbor, Albert Harris, was sometimes in on and frequently the victim of their escapades. I don't think the poor man was ever able to visit the outhouse in peace. Someone always dropped a cherry bomb down the vent pipe.

My mom worked in Emporia at the hospital and Aunt Betty was my day care provider. One day she was cleaning house and discovered a coiled snake at the back of the utility closet. She phoned Uncle Bud at his business in town at the welding shop screaming in panic that there was a rattlesnake in the closet. He broke a land speed record and several traffic laws covering the eight miles in less than ten minutes. Rushing into the house, he grabbed a shotgun from the back porch, ran to the closet and blasted away. He opened up a ragged dinner plate-sized hole in the floor of the closet, and then had some choice words to say to his wife when a closer examination proved the snake to be a coil of fringe off an old chair. Lucky for us because, if it had been a snake, he would have missed it completely.

On one of mom's days off, she and Aunt Betty decided to drive to town for groceries. Our car was a rickety old Model A Ford. It was a cold winter day so we were all bundled up because the heater didn't live up to its name, and the windows didn't quite crank to the top.

We were bouncing along old Hwy. 50, two narrow lanes, when a mouse appeared out of the upholstery, climbed onto Aunt Betty's lap, and perched on her knee. She screamed louder for the mouse than she had for the supposed rattler. The mouse didn't much appreciate the screaming, so it leapt onto the dash, ran over in front of mom, and sat there just inches from her nose because her short legs forced her to pull the seat as far forward as possible. She calmly rolled down the window and swiped the mouse out right into a passing truck. I can still see that right hand incased in one of dad's big work gloves as it slapped that mouse out the window. I thought she was the bravest woman on earth.

4

Dog vs. Sister

Mom, Jeri, and Queenie

Just before I began school, my parents present-ed me with another puppy. This dog was a better choice for a kid, and more appropriate for life on the farm. She was half collie, half German shepherd. We named her Queenie. She was a gem; smart, loyal, and beautiful, marked like a sable collie with shorter hair like a shepherd.

The old white farmhouse in Plymouth had only one bedroom and no indoor bathroom when we first moved in, so the first order of business was to convert the back porch into a bathroom. Since there was only one bedroom, the next project was to make a room for me at the top of the narrow stairs that led to what used to be the attic. The space made a perfect nest for a kid. An adult could stand fully upright only in the center of the room because of the steeply slanting roofline, but I was just the right size. I loved it...in the daytime. At night the two huge windows in the end walls allowed the moon or starlight to fill the room with creepy, clutching shadows as the trees outside swayed in the Kansas wind. Getting me to go to bed up there was always a struggle.

One summer night after all my delaying tactics had exhausted my mother's patience, dad escorted me up, plopped me into bed, pulled the sheet up to my chin, patted me firmly on the head, and ordered me to stay there and go to sleep. Queenie, my steadfast protector, lay curled up by the side of the bed. After I had sung all the verses to "Tumbling Tumble Weeds" three times and counted five or six hundred sheep, I dozed off. Suddenly, Queenie began to make low rumbling noises. My eyes flew wide open, and I could see a shadowy figure sitting in my little rocker. The phantasm was smoking, and every time it would take a drag, the tip of the cigarette would glow brighter. I was frozen with terror. I was too scared to move and even more afraid to stay still. Finally I began to scream. My parents came dashing up the stairs, wild eyed with concern. Of course they turned on the light, which revealed my Teddy bear sitting happily in the little red rocker with a lightning bug blinking on the end of his nose. Queenie was not growling; she had been snoring.

The little house on the prairie was cold in winter, and hot in summer. In winter dad kept the old wood stove in the middle of the living area piping hot with hedge and red elm. We were always cold on one side and lobster red on the other. In summer, on those 100-degree scorchers, the coolest place was the linoleum floor in the kitchen. On one such day, I was stretched on my back there watching mom fix lunch. She was wearing shorts—not her best look. She had inherited Grandma Lehnherr's short legs and cankles. (Grandpa often proclaimed that such legs looked best on a grand piano.) I looked up at her and said, "Mom, when I grow up, I sure hope I don't have legs like you!" Up until that moment my legs had been perfectly normal. God zapped me good. Lehnherr legs get you where you want to go, but they sure ain't purty.

When Queenie was about a year old, I learned I was going to have a brother or sister. This seemed unnecessary and arbitrary. I was six and the only child, but the days were accomplished and she was delivered: Mary Lisbeth, (Mary Beth for short) small, red, and useless. While she was being born, I was suffering in a darkened bedroom, quarantined with the red measles. I couldn't approach her or my mother until I was spot free.

Understandably, I was not thrilled with this situation. I remember standing in the doorway of the bedroom while the family at large was introduced to the newest member. My dad passed her piggybank, and everyone dropped in coins. I lobbed my plastic pig into the room from the bedroom door, but no one had any coins left. My grandpa saved the day by stuffing a dollar bill into the slot in my piggy's back.

This was just the beginning. Soon it became obvious that my parents valued MB more than my dog. I got a spanking for taking Queenie for a ride in the new baby carriage. There were shoutings about germs, hair, and fleas, but this was a huge injustice. My dog was surely better looking and certainly more intelligent than that squalling brat.

Other than the small matter of the sister, life in Plymouth was kid heaven. There was a tire swing in the elm tree, a cedar with conveniently arranged branches for climbing, and a muddy, forbidden creek a half mile away for frog catching and bullhead fishing. My friend, Nona, (a year younger and a head taller) lived less than a mile down the gravel road. We built forts and camps in the hedgerow behind her house. Nona's older brother Jerry destroyed our constructions as fast as we created them. We played "Roy Rogers" endlessly. Our biggest arguments were about who had to be Dale Evans. Her dog, Friday, and my Queenie accompanied us everywhere. He was a collie-type too and a valuable member of a working farm. He brought the cows in for milking every morning and evening. Nona's dad, Albert, cried for days when deaf old Friday didn't hear the tractor start, and Jerry accidentally backed over him.

Nona's mother Mary and my mom were childhood friends. The two of them belonged to Eastern Star, but could not afford formal dresses for one of the events, so they put an ad in *The Emporia Gazette*. My dad and Mary's husband Albert recruited an anonymous female accomplice to call Mom and Mary with directions to a house in town where they could inquire about scads of dresses, just the right sort of used formalwear. The residence, just south of the tracks on State Street, was infamous as the local whorehouse. Just imagine the conversation that ensued when Mom and Mary knocked on that door, and asked (as directed by the lady who responded to their ad) for Mrs. Easy.

Time came for another move, again without consulting me. This time we moved to Emporia to a white colonial on Peyton Street at the edge of town near the soybean plant. There was a huge yard complete with fishpond and a lovely arbor with a hammock and Paul Scarlet roses. Mary and I each had our own room upstairs. Queenie had ten acres to roam and a barn and chicken house to keep free of rats.

But problems with the sister just got worse. She became mobile and demanded to follow Queenie and me on all our adventures. My mother would always respond to her begging by saying, "Take her along." One day I had enough. I had made it to the edge of the pasture when she came to the gate. "Take me," she wailed.

"Go home, or I'll throw this rock," I threatened. She didn't, and I did, and for the only time in history, I hit what I aimed at. It was a small rock, and it made a small slit right at her hairline, dead center. Blood promptly oozed down her turned up nose. Screaming ensued, as did another flaking. I was heart sore and angry at the unfairness of it all. As usual, Queenie sympathized entirely.

Unlike Spike, Queenie did not kill farm animals or molest persons in uniform. Her only peccadillo was to roll in anything fetid and then go upstairs for a nap on my bed. I forgave her for fouling my sheets, and she forgave me for frequent baths. She learned to bring in my horse, catch escaped chickens without hurting them, jump a stick, sit up, roll over, speak on command, retrieve anything thrown, and shake hands. She loved to ride in the wagon (or the baby carriage), hunt rabbits and mice, kill snakes, and generally do whatever anyone asked her to do.

This was a problem the day MB directed her to jump a picket fence in the back yard. She missed and impaled herself on one of the pickets. The vet patched her up in short order, but it took me months to forgive my poor, contrite sister. I can still see the puddled tears in her big brown eyes.

Nevertheless, coldhearted, I set about getting even. I filled out her baby book. She often pouted because hers was empty while mine was crammed with pictures, cards, notes, family trees, snipped hair, finger and foot prints, lists of "firsts," cute sayings, and the beaded bracelet from the hospital with my last name. I began with a *National Geographic* article about a baby albino gorilla. This supplied most of the baby pictures. Queenie and an inkpad provided the footprint. In the "first haircut" spot went a hank of calf tail hair complete with a bit of manure. First word: "duh." Favorite food: "boogers." The result: another flaking from my mother.

The climax of all this animosity came when she was six and I was twelve. Our parents had gone out and left me in charge. I suggested we play amusement park and Mary was all for it. We took all the cushions off the chairs and couch and piled them at the bottom of the staircase. Then I put her in a cardboard box and shoved her down the stairs. "Whee!" She loved it. Do it again. "Whee!" But this time the box tipped over and she hit her head on the newel post at the bottom of the stairs. I thought she was dead. If I got a spanking for unlawful use of a baby carriage, pegging her with a rock, and filling out the baby book, what would happen if I had killed her? By the time I rushed to the bottom of the stairs, she was sitting up and blinking. There was a good-sized lump behind her ear, but no sign of death. She didn't even cry. Moreover, she didn't tell on me.

This was a huge turning point in our relationship. I realized I loved her and didn't want her to die. I saw that she valued my good opinion and wanted my approval. The fussing stopped and we have henceforth been buddies. She is a great person and I love her even though everything in her house matches and there is nothing in her garage but a car. Queenie and I both forgave her for the fence fiasco.

You are probably thinking at this point, that I was a terrible child. Well, you would be correct. During this time, Dad was working pretty steadily as a switchman on the Santa Fe. He worked from the "extra-board," which meant he could be laid off seasonally when there were not as many trains moving. For example, in winter there was less demand for cars full of wheat, cows, pigs, and sheep. I loved to watch him get ready for work in the winter. He would add layer upon layer until he was as round as Bob's Big Boy. Then he would turn to me, wink, and say, "A train might run through me, but it won't run over me."

Mom was working as an RN as the supervisor of the emergency room at St. Mary's Hospital in Emporia. She was a nurse back in the day when nurses looked like nurses: starched white uniforms with pearl buttons fastened on like cufflinks, starched caps that included a logo identifying the wearer's nursing school, white hose, and white "duty" shoes. A whiff of ether still takes me back to those times when mom would come home from attending an emergency with that odor clinging to her. This left Mary and me at home with a string of teen-age sitters. We had the freedom to get into all sorts of trouble. Queenie often stood in front of me barking her warnings that my current activities were unwise.

- Jumping off the chicken house roof with an umbrella was not a good idea. The result was a trip to the emergency room with a badly sprained ankle.
- Just because a tightrope walker in the circus could walk that wire does not mean a kid can safely replicate the act on top of a barbwire fence—another emergency run for stitches.
- Recreating an exciting rodeo bull ride with a reluctant 300 lb. calf was NOT a good idea either. I neglected to think that the

calf would not stop bucking when I yelled, "Whoa!" Possible concussion?

The final trip to the ER happened when Mom said, "If you show up here again, I will kill you." If you could have seen the fire in that pair of black Lehnherr dilated pupils, you would have believed her too!

Mary Beth also had her moments. When I look back at the old 8mm movies my dad took, I notice how goofy all of us were. Why would a group of reasonably intelligent people line up in rows and smile at the camera for a motion picture? Aside from a few waving hands, the only motion was MB. She was that blur that streaked by in front of the group. To this day, it is hard to get her to hold still. One day she crossed the road to visit Mr. Purttle. "Charlie," she warned, "I'm going to lock you in the shed." He laughed, silly man. She did. He was locked in most of the afternoon. His wife had to take the door off the hinges because MB threw the key in the fishpond.

We lived in the white house on Peyton Street until I was in high school. Just about every summer, Mary and I would travel by train to LA to visit my dad's sisters. We had passes because by then dad's job as a switchman had become full-time. We came home from one of these trips to find we had moved again. Big surprise. The house on Garfield never quite felt like home. Queenie and

I both missed the space and freedom, and I never really liked living in town.

Queenie lived for fourteen years and remains a star in my growing-up memories. She walked me to my first day of first grade at the old Plymouth School. I wore new jeans with stovepipe-sized cuff rolls, a plaid cowboy shirt, black and white saddle shoes, and a green plastic raincoat that still fit when I started junior high. My mother was always expecting me to grow, and I never did. I don't think any of my kid clothes ever fit before they wore out. (Mom made most of my clothes on her Singer Featherweight, bless her. And bless me because I wore them without complaint. I'll never forget the gauzy prom dress with orange roses.)

Twelve years after Queenie escorted me to my first day at Plymouth School, she walked me to my first day of college. Our house at 1214 Garfield was directly behind The College of Emporia campus. A scholarship and

EHS Prom 1961...Orange Roses!

work-study (fifty cents an hour) allowed me a fine liberal arts education at a bargain price. By then Queenie's joints were stiff and her eyes milky from cataracts. She be-

Queenie 1961

came incontinent and was in obvious pain. The day we decided she should be put down, I carried her to the back yard and took some pictures of her sweet face. The family mourned and for months missed stepping over her sleeping form when we went out the back door.

5

Family and Flint

Flint the Wonderdog

The best cure for missing a dog is another dog. It's not that you replace your lost friend; it's just that the heart always has room for more love and the mind for more memories. I heard that a rancher just west in Chase County had a litter of Australian shepherd border collie cross puppies for sale. I was about to buy my first dog. I drove to the Glendale Ranch near Lake Kahola. This is beautiful country. The idea that Kansas is flat is pure myth, at least as far as eastern Kansas is concerned. We have the Flint Hills. Here hills roll and bluestem grass abounds. This grass will fatten a cow more efficiently than any other grass on earth. There is space and wide blue sky, an occasional cottonwood or hedge tree along the draws, deer, wild turkeys, prairie chicken, quail, coyotes, and a colorful assortment of songbirds. Of course, summers sizzle and winters freeze, but springs and falls can be amazing, and in between, there are always climatological surprises. Weathermen love Kansas.

Seasonal change seasons life. Just when you think you cannot stand another snow flake and the brown grass is most depressing, a crocus blooms and whispers a promise of spring, and just when you think another gloomy April shower will bring on an outbreak of foot rot, the sun shines hot and drives you to the lake for a swim, and just when the hot wind has crisped the leaves on the redbud trees, a cold front sends you hunting for a sweatshirt, and just when the last leaf falls soggy to the ground, a soft snow blankets the bushes and soothes your soul. Don't tell anyone. I like the fact that a traffic jam in Kansas is two cars behind a combine.

Again I digress. In the Flint Hills, I found Flint, my Aussie. He was a blue merle with one blue eye and one brown eye and maybe the smartest dog I've ever known. He caught on to house training immediately, not one mess. During the summer, he sometimes went with me to work. I worked for the Rec Center as a playground supervisor. Neighborhood kids could attend six different playgrounds and participate in organized games and activities from summer movies to mankala tournaments. If my little Nash is still running, I'll bet to this day it reeks of sweaty kids. Flint loved to get in line with the kids and take his turn climbing the ladder to the top and sliding down the slippery slide.

He also went with me and my friends ice skating in the winter. He would stand in front of a skater and wait for her to pick up his tail. Then he would pull her at full speed across the ice. Once he attended a "woodsie" with a group of college friends. For the uninformed, a woodsie was a party with a bonfire, hotdogs, guitar led singing, and beer. Flint circled the fire helping himself from revelers cups. He got drunk.

Because Flint lived for almost fifteen years, he shared an important part of my life. He fell in love with my future husband right along with me, and welcomed each of our four children into the family.

Duane and I met in junior high but didn't begin seriously dating until the end of our senior year in high school. The first time I noticed him was in eighth grade English class. We were working on an assignment, and I kept feeling something tickle my back. I turned around to glare into horned rim glasses, Butch Waxed hair, and an amazing set of white teeth. Nerd! I returned to my essay. More tickling. Another dirty look. The tickling stopped, but when I got home and took off my white oxford cloth button-down shirt, SOMEONE had traced my bra straps in pencil on the back.

I remember clearly the moment when I began to see Duane as more than a friend. I went to his family's house on State Street to pick up a homework assignment after I had been absent from Mr. Price's chemistry class. His mom let me in the front door and told me to wait a minute, as Duane was getting ready for bed. He came downstairs all shiny and clean, smelling of soap, hair wet from the shower, wearing plaid jammies with the shirt buttoned up to his chin. I suddenly found him to be the cutest nerd I had ever seen.

After high school he went to Kansas State in Manhattan to begin work on a degree in Veterinary Medicine. I went across the backyard to begin studying to be an English teacher. I went to K-State on weekends. There are still people who think I went to college there. Duane was a good influence on my college career. In high school, I made decent grades, As and Bs except for typing. Miss Langley and I drove each other nuts. She always looked over my shoulder during timings, and I wanted to attack her Smith Corona with a sledgehammer. I'm pretty sure I hold the distinction of being the only person in the history of EHS to get a finger stuck between the keys during a time test. When Du made a 4.0 first semester, I decided I could do likewise. Besides, those weekends when I went to Manhattan were largely spent studying, well mostly studying.

After six short years we finally got engaged. One year later we were married. (As my dad walked me down the aisle, he gave me a bit of sage advice. "Don't ever wish for an elephant unless you really want one because that guy would arrange to get you an elephant.") Duane, Flint, and I moved to a charming (real-estate for small and old) duplex on Houston Street in Manhattan for his final year of Veterinary School. I taught seventh grade English at Manhattan Junior High just two blocks away. Flint stayed in the basement during the day. There was a landing at the top of the basement stairs and a door to the back yard. We would leave the outside door open and lock the screen. Flint would pee through the screen. Flint also enjoyed taking a bath. We didn't dare leave a tub full of water unattended.

Since my mom worked as a nurse as I was growing up, I learned to cook early. The women in my family, especially the grandmas, were all good cooks. My dad often picked up a wooden spoon too, and knew how to make fried chicken and a pretty mean chili. I saw no reason Duane could not be a help in the kitchen. One Friday evening we had invited another couple to join us for steaks. I knew I would be late getting home from school, so I asked Duane to bake the potatoes. "Just stick a fork in them and put them in the oven at 375 degrees for about an hour," I directed. When I got home, I was surprised to find each 'tater baking in the oven with one of our new stainless forks sticking out of it.

When Duane graduated from Vet school, we packed up our few early attic belongings and moved to San Antonio to begin his service in the US Air Force. This was 1967 back in the day of the draft. Duane had signed up with an early commission in the Veterinary Corps through ROTC. Vietnam loomed as a real possibility because health care for guard dogs demanded veterinarians there. But we were lucky, and he drew an assignment as the procurement and standardization vet for research animals at the School of Aerospace Medicine at Brooks Field in San Antonio, Texas.

As military bases go, Brooks was fortunately rather unmilitary. Duane's basic training was deferred because he was desperately needed at the research facility. ROTC really hadn't quite prepared him. He didn't even know how to put his lieutenant tracks on his uniform collar. I was afraid to go watch his first parade review because I figured he would march his unit up the bleachers.

I was just as unprepared to be a military wife. I decided to get to know other wives by writing for the base newspaper. They sent me to interview the general's wife. She was a gracious, refined lady who collected orchids and antiques. She invited me into her white-carpeted living room to sit on her white satin couch. She was telling me her story, and I was dutifully taking notes in my spiral notebook when a mouse ran across the carpet in front of my feet. I reacted like any self-respecting country girl. I stomped the sucker. Big mistake. Blood and guts on the white carpet. The general's wife managed to contain her horror, and I helped her clean up the mess after I picked Mickey up by the tail and took him to the white powder room for a dignified burial in a swirling white sea.

Not long after this incident, Mrs. General was hostess at the officer's club for a lovely brunch. All the officers' wives were invited, even the mouse masher. She had emptied her china cupboard to set the tables with fine dishes and sparkling crystal. She served champagne cocktails in elegant, bowl shaped antique stemware. As I took a drink, my glass broke right down the middle. There I sat with half the glass in my mouth and the other half in my hand and champagne staining the front of my pink silk blouse. This was my final invitation from the poor lady.

While we lived in San Antonio, Flint developed some interesting habits. He discovered his sexuality. We had a fenced back yard, but he was a leaper. We would monitor his location carefully, but when he got the urge to take off, the longer we forestalled his escape, the longer he would be gone when he finally made his break. Once he was gone for an entire week. We called the catcher and scanned the pounds. He finally came home, dragging a chain and filthy. There was a dead minnow caught in his coat.

After we had been in San Antonio about a year, Duane decided to take flying lessons. This required him to spend hours practicing, taking instruction, and studying instruments, maps, and regulations. Flint and I began to feel ignored. One evening before bed, I dressed up as a small aircraft with three strategically placed paper pinwheel propellers and ran screeching through the house as Flint chased and barked. We got his attention.

It was during our Texas tour that Miss Kristin Carol Henrikson joined our family. Flint had to learn to share, but he handled the new addition gracefully. The day we brought her home from the hospital, he walked into the nursery, stood on his hind legs without touching the crib with his front paws, and gave her a good long look.

Flint became a terrific family dog. We gave him lots of practice.

Thirteen months after Kristi, Beth was born, two years later, Todd joined the crew, and after a gap of five years, Sarah was born. Between the first two, Duane was discharged from the service and we returned to Emporia where he joined his dad's busy mixed animal practice. We settled into a little Cape Cod house in my old neighborhood on Garfield Street. (Of course, my parents no longer lived down the street...moved again.)

Flint was so patient with the kids. He would lie with them as they played in the sandbox and let them bury him in the sand. He continued to be an escape artist. The dogcatcher and he were on first name terms. He was an old friend in the neighborhood and would visit Mr. Howerton in the next block, taking along a tennis ball for games of fetch. He also went to the Brunners to check for steak bones whenever he smelled bar-becue. The man across the street was not so ac-cepting of his wanderlust. Once he sent an en-graved invitation to Flint's funeral.

Kristi, Flint, and Beth ready for another sandy burial

Ours was a busy household. The first three so close in age kept me spinning. They were cute, well-behaved kids, but I never seemed to keep ahead of them. They didn't disobey, but I just didn't always know what to tell them not to do. For example, it never occurred to me to tell them not to wax the kitchen floor with baby oil, or not to play tetherball with croquet mallets, or not to moisten the Gravy Train by dumping all 25 pounds in the sump pump.

Still I was proud of them. I about popped my buttons when Kristi said her first sentence, six whole words, "Why don't you just shut up?" And I loved Beth's astute critique of my beef stew after pushing it around for five minutes with her spoon, "Everything in here is wet." And Todd's sharp, scientific explanation to his grandmother's query in response to his inability to sit still, "No I don't have worms. Beth has worms. I have itchy boy spots."

One day Duane came home from work and asked why I didn't pick up some of the toys. (You'd think he would learn, but he still poses these kinds of questions: What did you do to your hair? Are you going to wear that? Is lasagna a casserole?) I took a deep breath and answered, "Have you ever spayed a dog and had someone come along and put the ovaries back in? Your work stays done. Mine does not. Now back off, Buster."

Duane worked hard. In the 70s most farmers had at least a few cattle, and a country vet had lots of after hours calls. His practice also serviced the local sale barn, which meant late sale nights with testing all the cattle that went through the sale. One of these "sale nights" happened to fall on Halloween. Duane didn't get home until after 10 p.m. so he missed all of the Trick or Treaters including his own kids. He was really bummed. I decided to cheer him up. I went into the bathroom, turned on the shower, stripped, wrote "Trick or Treat" on my belly, put on his old service raincoat and a paper bag with eyeholes on my head. Then I went outside and rang the doorbell. After a bit of a wait, he appeared at the door with the bowl of candy. I flashed him. For a couple of seconds, he didn't know who it was. Then he recognized some of the landmarks, and shut and locked the door. Fortunately I was able to make it to the back door before he locked it too.

I liked our little Cape Cod on Garfield, but I still longed for a place in the country where in addition to my dog, I could have a horse. To fill this void, we decided one Christmas to get the kids a pony. We could keep it at a friend's house in the country until we relocated. The O'Rear Welsh Pony Farm had a cute, tiny gray pony they were willing to loan us. Her name was Sunbeam. On Christmas morning there was a small saddle under the tree with a card reading, "Look out the window!" Outside was Sunbeam tied to the lamppost in the front yard. You can imagine the excitement.

In spite of city ordinances to the contrary, we decided we could keep Sunbeam in the garage over vacation before taking her to our friend's pasture. This was dandy until I came down with a raging case of flu. We were experiencing some very cold Kansas winter weather, but Kristi, Beth, and Todd insisted on going out to ride the pony. They would bridle and saddle her, then come in to drag me from my sick bed to go out and tighten the cinch. But the cold

Kristi, Beth, and one great Christmas present

kept driving them back into the house. After they warmed up, they would repeat the process. The fourth time, I told them "Enough! I'm sick. Don't get me out in the cold again!" In ten minutes they were back.

"Come tighten the cinch, mom."

"AAARGGG."

"It's OK. She's in the kitchen." Sure enough, there was Sunbeam flanked by Kristi and Beth, standing in front of the refrigerator with Todd holding down her tail in case she decided to poop.

When we found another Henrikson was coming, we decided we needed a bigger house. My mother asked me how many kids we were going to have. I told her I was not sure, as I still had not had my two planned ones. But I saw this as my chance to get back to country living. We began looking for a place to build on the edge of town. We finally found twenty acres three miles west just north of Highway 50. Flint was still with us to make the move, but by then he was fourteen years old and beginning to slow down. The day he made one of his breaks for freedom, and I was able to run him down was a tragic moment for him. I could see the pain in his eyes. I've never been known for foot speed or endurance.

We had lived in our new house for less than a month when I found him at the end of our drive, apparently lost. His eyesight was about gone, and he didn't know where he was. Dr. Duane knew the time had come to put him down. We put it off for another month, but Flint had stopped eating and hardly moved from his bed in the garage. One of the other doctors in the practice gave the injection and we buried him in the pasture by the plum thicket.

6

The Country Life

The home on the prairie

Duane had his doubts about moving to the country, but he took to it like fruit flies to ripe bananas, building fences, planting trees, cutting brush, tilling a garden spot. He even got into bee keeping. Two or three times a year, mild-mannered veterinarian disappeared into the tack room and came out as BEEMAN. You've seen the outfit: white coverall, helmet with net, gauntlet gloves, smoker in hand, ready to "work the bees." I, on the other hand, am allergic. I swell when stung.

He calls to me from the beehives, "Help, I need a big bowl. This comb is cracking and the honey is spilling."

I answer, "I'll get stung."

"No," he promises, "I'll make sure to brush all of the bees back into the hive." Well he missed one. It flew up and stung me through my shirt right on the left boob. I threw the bowl at him and ran to the house for aloe and Benadryl. When he came in later, I showed him my hugely lopsided chest. "Just a minute," he quipped, "I'll go get another bee."

The bees prospered. Time came for the hive to divide. When this happens, the bees swarm. They raise a second queen, and half the workers escort her from the hive to fly away to find a new home. Duane was ready for them. He had spent weeks pounding together new frames for a new hive while the rest of us were trying to watch *Magnum PI* or *Laugh In*.

One hot, still afternoon we heard a buzzing as a cloud of bees hovered above the lawn. I waved Duane off the mower just as the swarm took off. "What do I do?" he shouted.

"I think I read somewhere that a loud noise will make them settle," I answered. He ran into the barn and came out banging two garbage can lids like giant cymbals while running after the bees. He chased them down the drive, across the road, and disappeared over the horizon to the west. After about thirty minutes, I told Todd to get in the truck and go find his father.

When they came home, my out of breath hubby gasped, "I lost them at Plymouth." That's six miles away. He finally gave up on the bee project after they chased him out of the garden while he was tilling the potato patch. He just left the tiller there chugging away until it ran out of gas.

I hope, dear reader, that you do not get the impression I do not love and respect my husband. He is simply one of the best people I know—an amazing veterinarian, an upright citizen of Emporia, a loving father and husband. He is smart, handy, creative, and kind. He tells me that, except for leaving the bread sack open, he is perfect. Infuriatingly, he is just about right on that one. He is also funny. A sense of humor is a requirement around here. Some of his funny is intentional. Some just comes out of his pores. He is a master of the mixed metaphor:

- When he and his partner at the clinic were discussing the purchase of a new truck, the partner asked, "Should we take the 10% discount or the free financing?" Duane answered, "It's a flip off." No, a trade off, or a flip of a coin. This is a flip off...see me demonstrate a one finger salute.

- I am complaining about losing a favorite earring. "Forget it," he says. "It's water over the bridge." No dear, water over the dam, under the bridge.

- Comment made after struggling up a muddy two-track in the old truck to reach a paved road: "It sure is good to be back on good old terra cotta." Firma?

Also, as a dog and horse lover, it was really a smart move to marry a veterinarian.

When we built our home on Rt. 5, we started with a wheat field: no grass, no trees. One day when I was out for a horseback ride, I noticed some Kentucky coffee bean trees growing in the road ditch less than a mile from our house. I told Duane about them and he called the landowner for permission to dig a couple: one for us, and one for some friends, who were also treeless. We planted the tree by the front walk, staked it properly and watered it diligently through the fall and winter. The next spring, we waited for signs of life. The friends' sister tree had six inches of new leaves. Ours, sadly, remained bald. I told Duane to pull up the tree, but he insisted on giving it more time.

June 5th, our wedding anniversary came and the tree was obviously lifeless. I went to the local nursery to buy our traditional gift for each other, a tree for the yard. By jingo, they had some small coffee bean trees, one of which was exactly the same size and arrangement of branches as our dead one. I bought it and took it home, pulled up Dead Fred, and put the new tree carefully into the hole, replacing the stake and dirt exactly. Then I just waited. For three days Duane passed the tree without noticing the flourishing new growth. I remained silent. The fourth morning he stopped, turned on his heel, and came bursting back through the door. "Come look at this! It's a miracle! Look at the leaves! How could this happen over night!"

"You're right," I answered. "It's a miracle!"

At noon he came home dragging his partner and two lunch buddies with him to show them the miracle tree. They stood in mild bemusement wondering if the poor man had lost his mind, tearing up over a silly tree. A week or so later, he was out cleaning up the trash pile and found Dead Fred among the litter. He picked it up and came stomping toward the house. I locked the doors and ran around inside yelling over and over, "It's a miracle, it's a miracle!"

———

The kids joined 4-H and the next generation of Henrikson dogs belonged to them, not me. Each of them had a dog as a project, training them in obedience and showmanship. Kristi's dog was a sweet black and tan Australian shepherd named Waltzing Matilda, "Tillie." She was a terrific showmanship dog, and loved all the attention involved in getting prepared for the dog show. She would even run upstairs after her bath and bring down a bandana for Kris to tie around her neck. That old saw of dogs being like their owners was surely true of this duo. Kristi too loves to please and doesn't know a stranger.

Beth's dog was a dignified Doberman named Raven. She did well in obedience and was a gentle, stoic friend to anyone who wanted one but was especially devoted to Beth. She was a smart dog, but found tricks beneath her. She thought playing fetch was stupid. She would bring the ball once, but if you threw it again, you were on your own. In addition to the dog project, Todd was enchanted with rocketry. After one of his dramatic countdown launches, the rocket drifted beyond the woods behind our house. Everyone looked, but no one could find the missing rocket. The next day, Raven brought it to the house after her morning rounds. Beth was crazy about that dog. She had a t-shirt with "I love Dobermans" printed on the front. That shirt never made it to a drawer. It went from back to washer to dryer, to back and back. When Raven died at age ten from cancer, we buried her next to Flint by the plum trees. I was doing just fine until I looked out the next morning and saw Tillie sleeping by the grave.

Todd wanted to adopt every orphan pup that came to the clinic. He finally talked his dad into a border collie (she bordered on being a collie) that he named Tux. Tux was a challenge even for patient Mr. Todd. This was a dog of limited learning power, possibly the only stupid border collie on the planet. She learned "sit" and thought that sitting was the correct response to any command. And she would look up at Todd with this "ain't I good" expression. Todd always brushed and polished her perfectly for showmanship, because he knew his chances were not good in obedience. At one show, the judge complimented him on the condition of Tux's coat. She asked if he bathed her every day. Todd said, "No, but she swims in the lagoon pretty often."

Finally Todd retired Tux and bought a beautiful Viszla he named Anna. Viszlas known as Hungarian pointers, are a very old hunting breed from Eastern Europe, sometimes pictured on me-

Anna and Todd ready for the show ring

dieval tapestries. Anna proved to be great on upland game birds, a wonderful pet, and a fine show dog, taking top prizes at the Kansas State Fair. At one of the shows, she was completing the long down, an exercise where the handler gives the "down/stay" command, then exits the area to a place out of sight of the dog. The dog must stay there alone for five minutes at which point the handler returns to "release" the dog to heel. Anna had been perfectly still for four and a half minutes when a chattering sparrow flew down from the rafters and lit about three yards in front of her. In ultra-slow motion, she rose to her feet and struck a perfect bird-dog point. The crowd cheered, but Anna and Todd lost out on a top purple ribbon. One litter of her puppies paid for Todd's first semester tuition at K-State. Sadly, Anna disappeared. We searched for her, called the pound, notified the sheriff, put ads in the paper and on the radio offering a reward. My theory is that someone invited her into their car and took her. She was always eager to go hunting, and would have gone with anyone dressed and equipped for a hunt. All of us missed her, of course, especially Todd.

Todd talked us into keeping one of Anna's pups. We named him Max, but he thought his name was Dammit Max (no relation to Dammit Skipper, Get Your Ass in Here). He was the ultimate retriever, but he retrieved objects into the hayloft. Lay down

a screwdriver, hayloft. Drop your sunglasses, hayloft. Lean the rake against the fence, hayloft. Once
he picked up the rope on a ground-tied horse and
tried to lead it up the stairs into the hayloft.

The plan was for us to keep Max until Todd was
settled into his own place. But Todd just kept going to school. He became a veterinarian, and then
did more schooling to become a veterinary radiol-
ogist. When he had a place for Max, the dog was
getting pretty old. Todd took him for a weekend,
and Max stopped eating and developed a cough.
Ironically, a radiograph proved he had lung cancer. We brought him home and he made a small
rally, but the disease was advancing quickly. Again
we had to face that moment. The little graveyard
beside the plum thicket was getting to be quite
the pet cemetery.

Since Sarah arrived after the first rush, she
inherited clothes, dogs, and horses from the first
three. They all claim she is hopelessly spoiled.
She just smiles. Somehow she was born with this
amazing sweet, refined, placid disposition. Sarah
could have been prissy, but the others took care of
that. She complained once that the dogs had gone
to the bathroom in the garage. Beth informed her
that dogs do not go to the bathroom; they shit.

Sarah has always loved to shop. She even en-
joys shopping with and for me. When she was
about four, the two of us went to the local Pennys
to get me a new swimsuit. Old Blue had given out.

I always went to Pennys for swimwear because of the mirrors **inside** the dressing rooms. With Sarah's help, I chose three or four suits to try. "Can I go in the dressing room with you?" she asked. I found this request to be amusing, as at this point in my life, I had not taken a bath in private for about ten years. I had recently considered replacing the bathroom door with a turnstile..."sure, why not," I answered.

She composed her pretty, delicate features, widened the big brown eyes, and said with complete sincerity, "I promise I won't laugh."

Sarah continued the tradition of dogs at the fair. Her pup was a tiny minpin named Gabby. He was smart and did well in the dog shows, but he was constantly getting into rows with the local wildlife. A raccoon nearly took off his left ear. A direct hit in the face from a harried skunk left him

Gabby and Sarah scrubbed and polished for the Lyon County Fair

half blind for a week. He was nearly disemboweled by a coyote. After each of these incidents, Duane did a masterful job of putting him back together, but he began to look a bit Frankensteinish: one ear sat too far up on his head and scars zagged across his little body like stitches on grandma's crazy quilt. He met his end when he took on a bobcat. We buried what was left of him by the plums in the pasture.

Our kids were growing up, and they continued to find creative ways to express themselves. On Father's Day one spring, the four of them went together to buy their dad some new jogging shorts. We had tried to throw away the old green ones, but he kept dragging them out of the trash and wearing them even though the ragged lining sagged below the hemline like tattered underwear. When Duane came home that evening, he found an impressive ceremony awaiting him. The four kids and their four dogs stood in a reverent circle around the worn-out shorts, recently drenched with lighter fluid and burning nicely, as Todd played taps on his trombone.

7

Dogs of the Empty Nest

Jane watching TV

Time passes. In a blink Kristi, Beth, Todd, and Sarah were grown and off making lives of their own. The day I took Sarah to Kansas State to begin college, I arranged to meet a friend on my way home to buy my first dog since Flint died. I chose a Jack Russell terrier. Her name was to be Jane Russell. I had done some homework and knew what I was getting into. Some claim the breed is misnamed. They should be called Jack Russell terrorists. Terriers are bred to be busy; easily distracted by anything that moves, aggressive toward varmints, independent thinkers, and quick, strong, athletic, and stubborn. The Jack Russell is the ultimate terrier. Jane, the ultimate Jack Russell, was only eight weeks old when I brought her home, and she could leap up on the couch from a flatfooted start. Her quick turns and sprints meant she could outrun Dammit Max. She learned to play fetch with a knotted sock in about three minutes and would never bother a sock without a knot in it. (If you were to see my laundry room, bedroom floor, or TV room, you would understand the importance of this fact.)

She watched television. Milo and Otis was her favorite movie. If anyone yelled, "Dogs on TV," she would rush in and sit up in front of the screen until the dog scene was over. Jane loved to make up her own games. If she could not get one of her humans to throw her tennis ball, she would take it into the hayloft and drop it down the stairs or out the loft door, then retrieve it herself. She also played soccer solo by rolling a soccer ball full speed around the yard and pasture. Jane pursued a packrat into the engine of our car and did $800 worth of damage to the wiring.

Jack Russells are smart, spunky, cute, and engaging. Unfortunately, they are so dedicated to "varmint" hunting that they are often self-destructive. Many do not reach a ripe old age because they get trapped in holes trying to dig out a rabbit, dive from a moving car window when they spot a squirrel, or run in front of a passing car when chasing a cat. When she was just five years old, she was with Duane out by the road helping him fix fence. She flushed a rabbit and was killed by a passing car as she chased the rabbit across the road. I cried.

I missed having a dog around, but it took about a year before I could look for another dog. I couldn't bear the thought of another Russell so I decided to look for a corgi. I found Miss Jones. She's Welsh, you know. What a cute little ball of fluff. The Pembroke Welsh corgi is the smallest herder. I quickly understood why The Queen is so crazy about them. They smile, chuckle, bounce, fetch, herd anything that moves, and clean

Jones taking a tennis ball time out

themselves like cats. The word "corgi" in Welsh translates to "dwarf dog." In my mind, they have to be the favorite dogs of Hobbits.

Jones loved to go walking and was a perfect lady on the leash. She brought me the paper. I was never alone. She followed me from room to room. She liked to be boarded at the clinic when we went on vacation because all the vets, techs, kennel cleaners, and secretaries loved her and took her on errands to the post office or to make bank deposits.

When Jones was just short of her tenth birthday, she suddenly stopped being her usual bouncy self. Duane took her to the clinic for tests, which showed her to be suffering from lymphoma. Chemotherapy bought her about six months. When the symptoms came back, the second round of treatment failed, and the sad moment came when we added another small grave to the little cemetery near the plum trees.

The fact is, memories of Miss Jones always remind me of Skipper. Perhaps she will be the one my grandchildren remember as their first favorite dog. Perhaps memories of her will jog recollections of grandpa and grandma, their house in the country, the funny stories they used to share at the dinner table, the joy of laughter, and the warm security of aunts, uncles and cousins who love them without condition. Perhaps Miss Jones will foster in them that amazing bond between a person and

a well-loved dog. Who knows? Perhaps they will
also grow to measure time by the lives of their favorite dogs.

8

Present Tense

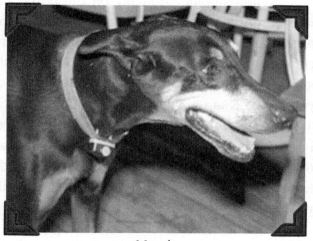

Maude

About four years ago, Duane and I found ourselves pack leaders for four dogs. This happened gradually. We began with a new Doberman puppy. Named her Maude. After we had owned her for about six months, the breeder called. "How's the new dog?" he asked.

"Just terrific!" I answered.

"What did you name her?"

"Maude."

Silence..."Why did you name her that?"

"Because she's a Maude."

"Is she a good watch dog?"

"No, she's a Maude. Mostly she leans on legs, looks soulfully into eyes, and sleeps curled up in the old brown chair. She's quiet, obedient, tidy, and sweet. We love her."

When she sits stoically on the porch and looks intently at visitors, there is no need for barks, growls, or teeth. Strangers honk the horn. Friends come up and pat her on the head as she leans into their leg and looks soulfully into their eyes. Once Duane sent the kennel boy from the clinic to our house to pick up his forgotten cell phone. Maude was asleep in the brown chair, home alone. The boy walked in, picked up the phone, saw Maude and froze. She did not wake up. That's Maude. We love her.

Gertie

Gertie is our second Welsh corgi. She is tri-colored, essentially black and tan with white belly, a stripe down her nose, half a white ruff, and white legs. She is needy. She wants to be held, but does not fit in a lap, so when she jumps into a lap, she is still for about five seconds and then begins squirming like a stranded beach master bull seal. She is not supposed to jump up on visitors, but does it anyway. She sits up so she is closer to a pat on the head. She is quite herdy. She tries to herd cars, mowers, hoes, brooms, the other dogs, people, and cats: anything that moves.

She tries really hard to talk. When I won't move in the direction she desires, she looks me in the eye and gives out verbal directions. Unfortunately, I do not speak corgi—or Welsh. She has those huge corgi ears, and every time anyone says the word, "food," those ears fly into the full upright position. Like me, she loves to eat, and should not eat as much as she loves. She stays at the right weight because we limit meal size and snacks...if only I had a feeder with such control. Gertie is steadfast and loyal. She follows me faithfully everywhere I go. She is great on the leash and fun to take walks with. We love her.

Eli

Dobes are Dr. Duane's favorite breed. They are stoic, and intuitive: they seem to understand that the vet is trying to help them when they are in pain. Our friends Jan and David Traylor are fellow Doberman lovers. In fact, Dave and I travelled together to buy his dog Mattie and our Maude. They are sisters. We each picked a pup. He put a red collar on his and I put a blue collar on ours, and we installed them in a big carrier in the back of his van. The pup with the red collar yapped all the way home. David accused me of switching the collars. I told him I had not, but would have if the other one were doing the yapping. Duane spayed Maude, but Mattie had a nice litter of purebred puppies. The Traylors were generous and kind and gave one pup (Lenny) to our son Todd and another (Eli) to daughter Sarah. When Sarah and her family moved to a home with a small yard, she gave Eli, then three years old, to us. When she loaded him into our car, he began to jump around from front to back like an idiot. I yelled at him to sit. Sarah said, "Mom, he is not used to that tone of voice."

"Give him a week!" I retorted.

We have had Eli for four years now. He is a lovely dog. He sings with the coyotes. He kills skunks and possums and leaves them for us on the deck. He does a terrific cold Doberman act, complete with chattering teeth, that works to get into the house, unless the temperature is above 70 degrees, or he smells like a skunk.

He and Maude used to sit together stoically on the porch and stare intently in unison at visitors. Like Maude, he is no threat, unless he smells like a skunk. We love him even when he smells bad.

Jazzy

Our veterinarian daughter, Sarah called one day and asked if we would like to adopt a JRT female six years old. Her family just added a new member, and the dog was too barky: kept waking the baby. It took Jazz about three weeks to take over. One would expect no less from a Jack Russell Terrorist. The Doberman avoids her, and whenever Gertie tries to herd her, she gets her plow cleaned.

Jazz is too cute, black and white with a half and half face and one ear that lops while the other signals a permanent left turn. She trots around with jaunty self-assurance and has laid claim to a convenient chair in each room. She came with a cozy bed, which Gertie damn well better stay out of if she knows what's good for her. She has invented a game called "Toss the Rock." This involves finding a smooth brown rock...not one of those chalky white ones. She brings said rock to a receptive looking human and flips it at a foot. If human does not pick up rock and toss it, barking ensues. There are two possible problems with the game: 1) human gets bored and refuses to toss the rock properly i.e. throws it into the bird bath or, 2) Gertie intercepts the throw and takes off for the back yard. All's fair in canine sibling rivalry.

She is beginning to tone down the barking. She is beginning to come when called. She now only chases cats when no one is looking. She has learned to sit on command and has stopped licking the CLEAN dishes in the dishwasher. We are learning to love her.

Town Dogs

We recently moved into town. We love our new all-on-one-floor home with the beautiful view of the golf course. It was in no way easy to leave our country home, but we had lots of help from our kids. The place just got to be too much work: lots of upkeep of gardens and too much house. We no longer need five bedrooms. We miss dark night stars, sunsets through the hedge trees, wild turkeys in the tomatoes, and our long time neighbors, Ann and David Eldridge. We don't miss gravel roads, mud and dust, grasshoppers, weeds, and power failures. Duane has retired so we are embracing the chance to travel.

Of course the dogs, Eli, Gertie, and Jazz, moved with us. Sadly we lost Maude to cancer about a month before we moved. Duane and I are in our 70s now, which means we have outlived some very special dogs. Maude was one of the best. We buried her ashes with the others beside the plum thicket in the north pasture. It is appropriate that she stay. This was the only home she knew for her 10 years with us.

As we were transferring our lives to the new place, we would bring the three amigos with us to give them a chance to adapt to this new house. At first, they would sniff around, mark trees, go in and out with us as we brought in beds, tables, chairs, rugs, books, and boxes. After a bit, they would all three line up beside the car, waiting to go "home." When we finally spent the first night in the new digs, they were pretty well adapted. There was a little pacing and restlessness, but when we went back to Route 5 to pick up the last load (most of which should have gone to the dump), they ran around a bit, then lined up beside the car to go "home." Smart.

Recently we saw a new side to Eli. We had an "invisible fence" installed before we moved, an easy transition from the country as we also had one at our old house. All three dogs were resting and watching cars go by when three stray dogs approached from the west. Eli rose to his feet and showed his teeth. Hackles rose from nose to tail. The tan pit bull and his burly companions decided to detour around our yard. I have often thought there was not an aggressive bone in Eli's body, and that he would stand happily aside as a potential robber hit me with a shovel. Perhaps I've misjudged the old boy.

So this brings us to now. All three of our town dogs are 10+ years of age. I'm one of those people who lives pretty much in the present, although you can see I love remembering the past. At this point in my life, I am so grateful for each new day. We have seven amazing grandchildren, five of them within walking distance and the other two just an hour's drive away. We also have three grand-dogs who come to visit for holiday dinners with their families. I must admit I wouldn't mind living long enough to continue watching the grandkids growing and changing. Of course, I would also hope for another dog or two to brighten any golden years we have left. I simply cannot imagine a life not measured in dog years.

Postscript

Of course this merry, dog-trot through my life is not the whole story. None of us reaches our seventies without experiencing sad, even tragic moments. One lesson that keeping pets teaches us (unless you have a fondness for parrots and Galapagos turtles} is that life is short, and shit happens. Life gets messy. But the joys of having a dog outweigh the unpleasant chore of picking up the poop. Perhaps the hard parts make the joyful parts more joyful. The birth of a grandchild balances the death of a grandparent.

Watching the lifecycle of a beloved pet run its course prepares us for the inevitable repetition of that pattern in our own lives. Duane and I have experienced the pattern with grandparents, parents, siblings, aunts, uncles, cousins, and treasured friends; some with long lives, some we felt, gone much too soon. I am reminded of a moment when granddaughter Sydney and I were leaving the rest home after visiting Duane's mother, Ruth. I said to her, "Well Syd, I'm next."

She smiled up at me and replied, "Yup, and then Mom...and then me." But there's lots of good stuff yet to be.

I hope you won't be upset that I have kept the stories sunny and funny. It just seemed the right slant for a waggy dog sort of tale. Dogs, it seems, have a talent for keeping positive.

Joy to you in all you do. Love rules. JH

Acknowledgments

As always, when a book happens, there are people to thank. I must begin with my dear husband, Duane, because he kept my computer on task and helped by searching through piles of family photos to find just the right ones. Mostly, he quietly supports my addiction to this second career of mine. My buddy, Sharon Stephens, is a steadfast, straightforward editor who offers honest and helpful criticism. Sharon Stewart, Jan Traylor, and Martha Jones read early drafts and assured me that I was on the right path. My publisher, Sherri Rowe claimed that my stories made her laugh out loud.

I would also like to thank my family, immediate and extended, who have supported me in countless ways, but especially for being the assorted nuts and chews that they are, and for branding my life with humor and love.

And perhaps, most importantly, I thank each of my dogs, for just being dogs, those amazing bundles of loyalty and devotion that have always been happy to see me come home.

—Jerilynn Jones Henrikson

Other Books by Author

Teddy the Ghost Dog of Red Rocks is a historical fiction chapter book for upper elementary about the family of William Allen White, Pulitzer Prize winning journalist from Emporia, Kansas. The story is narrated by the ghost of the White's fox terrier who is still a presence in the family home, Red Rocks. Winner of KART Kids Book List.

Grandma's Prairie Patchwork a Kansas Color Book features iconic Kansas images narrated by a friendly Kansas granny. Staying inside the lines is not required!

Raccoons in the Corn is the tale of Farmer B and his efforts to save his precious sweet corn from marauding raccoons. This story is for middle elementary.

Prairie Tales the Wispers, Grones, and Ponders features three story poems about mythical inhabitants of the tall-grass prairies. This is a fun "read-to-me" book for littles, or read it yourself stories for more independent readers.

Bad Cat is a story for primary level readers about ornery cat, BC, and his ornery antics. Little ones enjoy playing "Find the Mouse," as bigs do the reading.

———

Look for *Teddy* at Rowe Publishing, and local booksellers, or the author's website www.prairiepatchwork.com. Other stories available also on author website.

CPSIA information can be obtained
at www.ICGtesting.com
Printed in the USA
LVOW03*0734091116
512260LV00005B/14/P